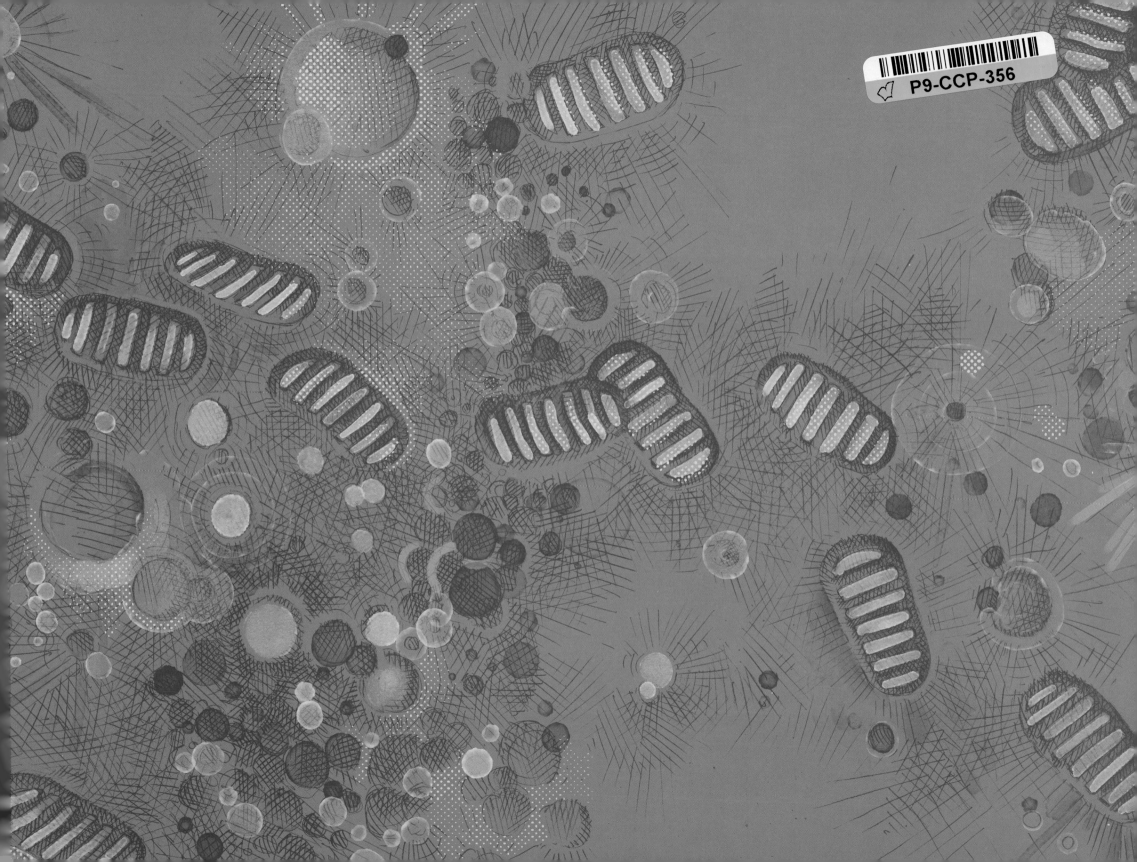

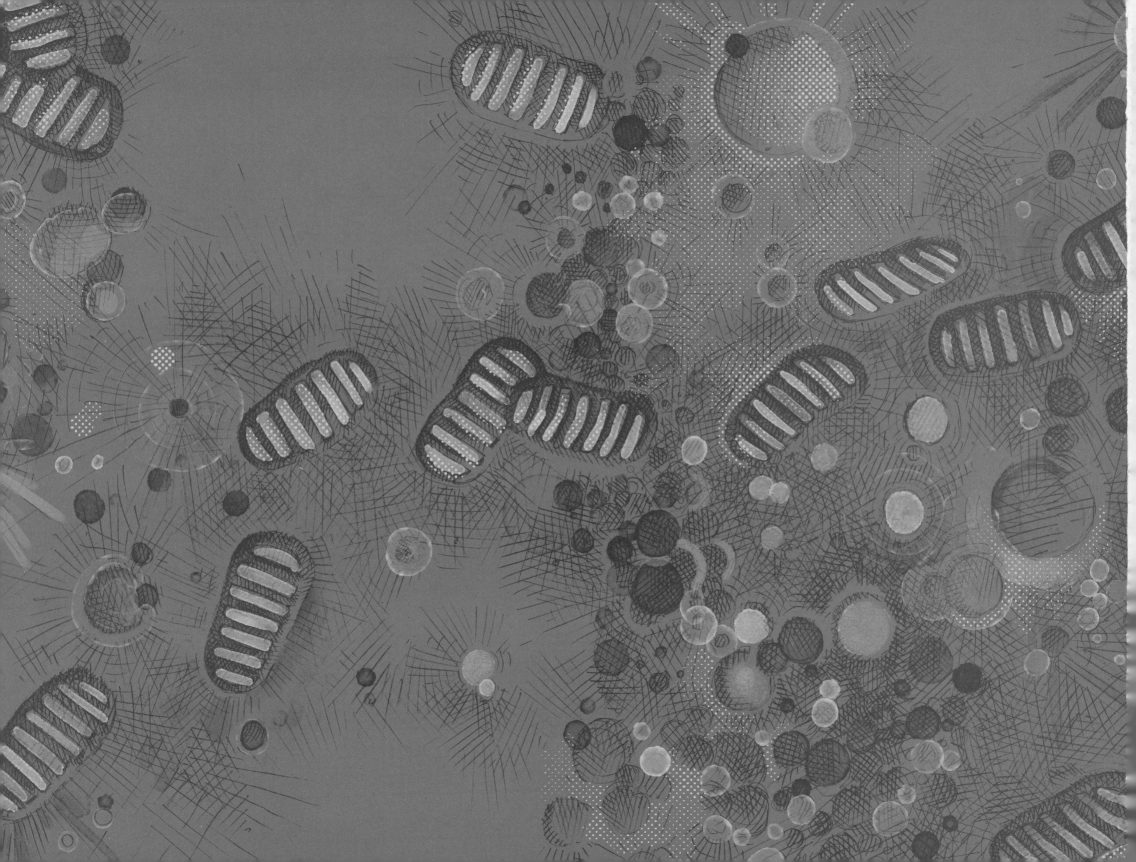

THE TRUE STORY OF ALAN BEAN

THE ASTRONAUT WHO
Painted the Moon

WRITTEN BY
DEAN ROBBINS

ILLUSTRATED BY
SEAN RUBIN

ORCHARD BOOKS
NEW YORK
AN IMPRINT OF SCHOLASTIC INC.

"My paintings record the beginnings of a quest
never to end, our journey out among the stars."

—Alan Bean

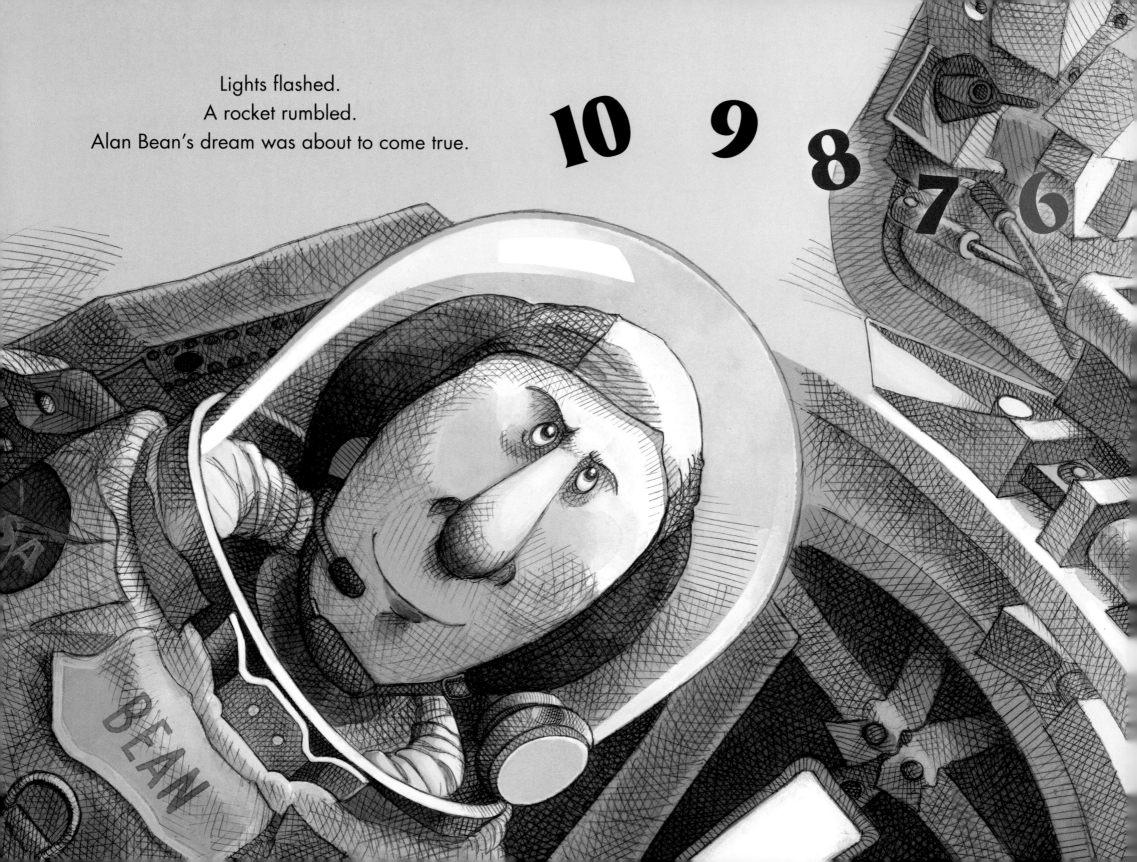

Lights flashed.
A rocket rumbled.
Alan Bean's dream was about to come true.

10 9 8 7 6

5

4

3

2

1 . . .

The rocket roared off the launchpad!

Alan shook in his heavy spacesuit.
The other astronauts were shaking, too.
Richard Gordon flipped switches on the control panel.
"That's a lovely liftoff!"
Pete Conrad shouted over the noise.

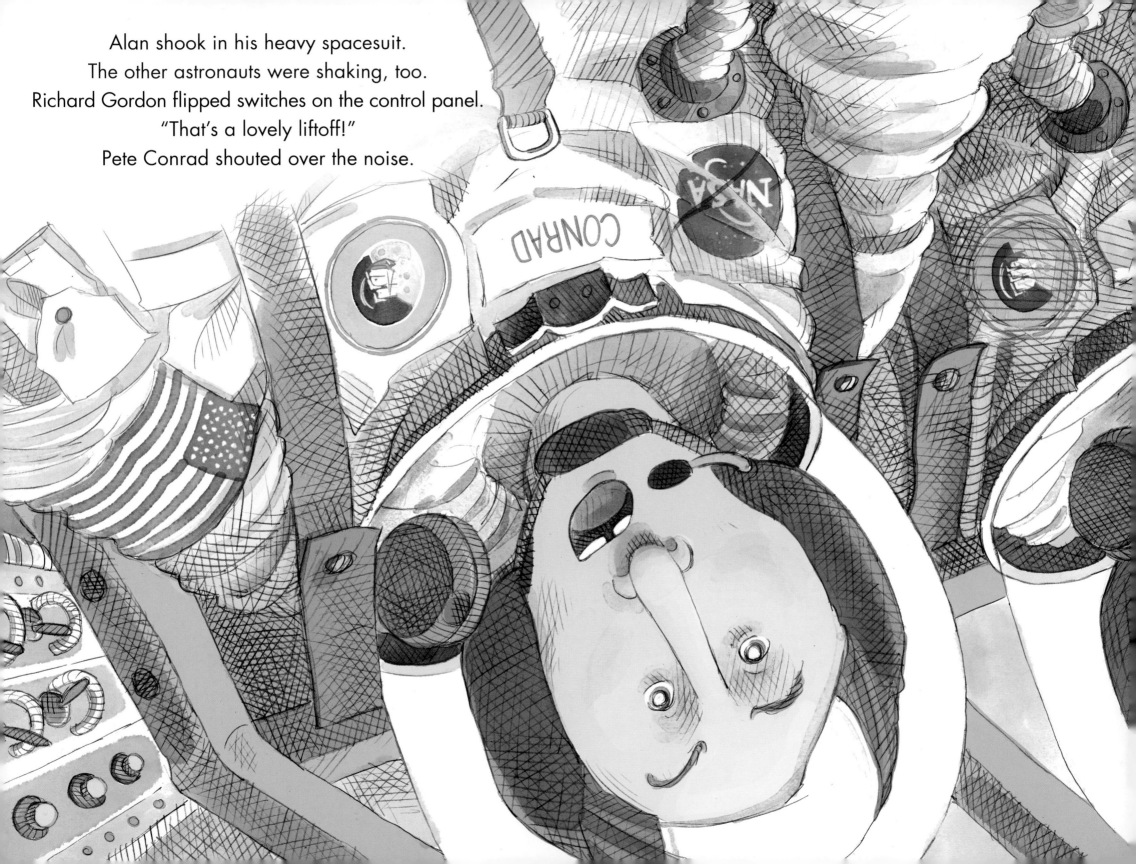

The shaking stopped as the spacecraft gained speed.
Alan was in outer space!
He had trained for so long as an astronaut and
a scientist, and soon he would walk on the Moon!

Alan gazed out the window, marveling at the shapes and colors in space.
The sky turned to black.
The Earth was a blue-and-white ball glowing in the darkness.
The Moon was many shades of gray.
Its mountains and craters seemed bigger the closer he got.

Alan loved to think about the way things looked.
As a boy, he made model airplanes to hang in his room.
Green for the wings.
Red stripes for the tail.
Yellow stars along the sides.

He dreamed of being
a brave pilot himself one day.

Alan volunteered for navy flight training.
He learned to take off . . .
soar through the air . . .
and glide in for a smooth landing.

The Earth looked breathtaking from the cockpit.
The white clouds above.
The green fields below.
The blue all around.
Alan wished he could paint what he saw.

He found an art class to teach him about patterns and forms.
Alan dabbed his brush on canvas to paint a vase of flowers.
His flowers didn't look exactly real, but he didn't want them to.
They were brighter and bolder than real ones because he let his imagination take over.

The painting showed how stunning the flowers looked through Alan's eyes. How they made him feel.

The spacecraft flew 240,000 miles in four days.
The Moon was so close Alan could see valleys and ridges.
He and Pete got ready to walk on a new world!

Alan strapped on an oxygen pack so he could breathe outside.
He stepped through the hatch to the most amazing sight.

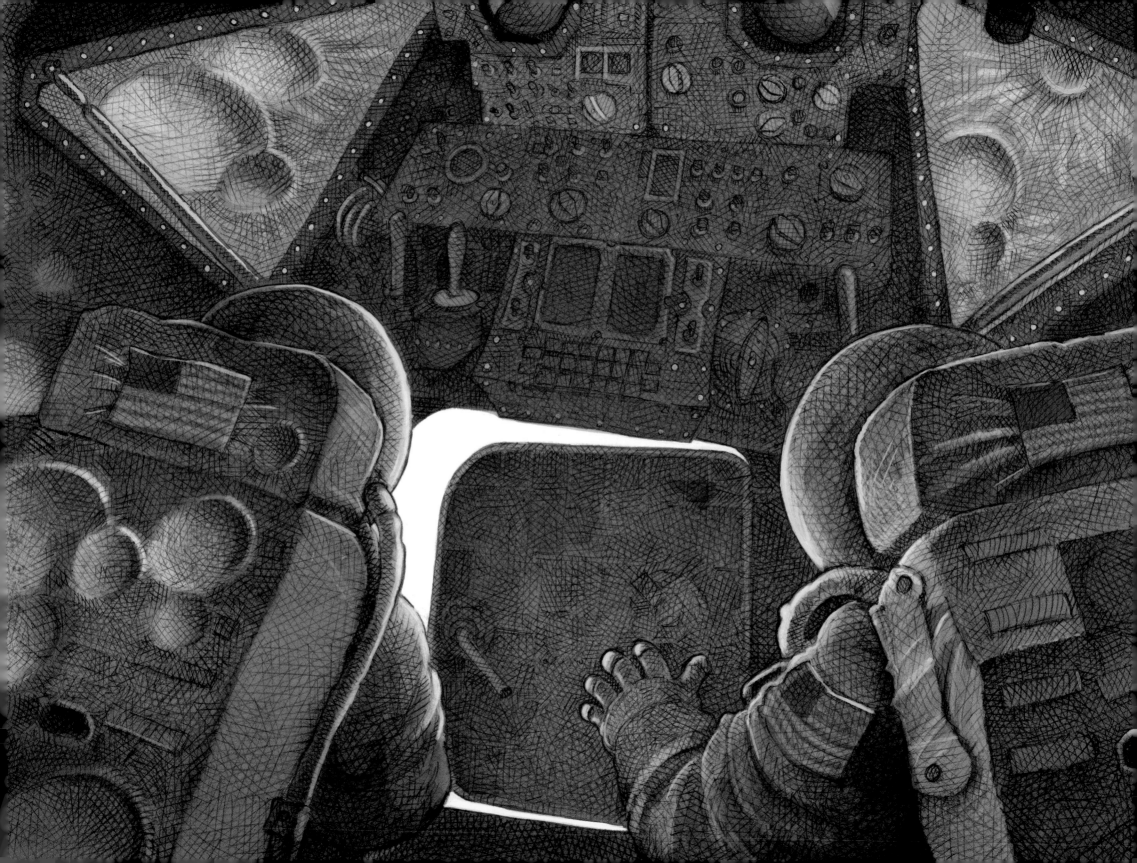

The Moon was barren,
but also beautiful in its own way.
Gray dust as far as he could see.
Thousands of black craters.
Hard white sunlight.
And everything perfectly still.

Alan and Pete pushed a red, white, and blue American flag into the dust.

Alan puzzled over the strangeness of outer space.
He and Pete took dozens of photographs.
They set up scientific experiments
to measure the Moon's soil and gases.

Even in his spacesuit,
Alan was much lighter than on Earth.
He had fun bouncing around on his tiptoes.

He could run and run without getting tired.
His boots made deep marks where no one
had stepped before.

Alan was super-strong in the Moon's
gravity. He threw a rock and watched
it go up, up, up.

Would it ever come down again?

The three astronauts zoomed back to Earth at 25,000 miles an hour. They splashed into the Pacific Ocean to end their awesome adventure.

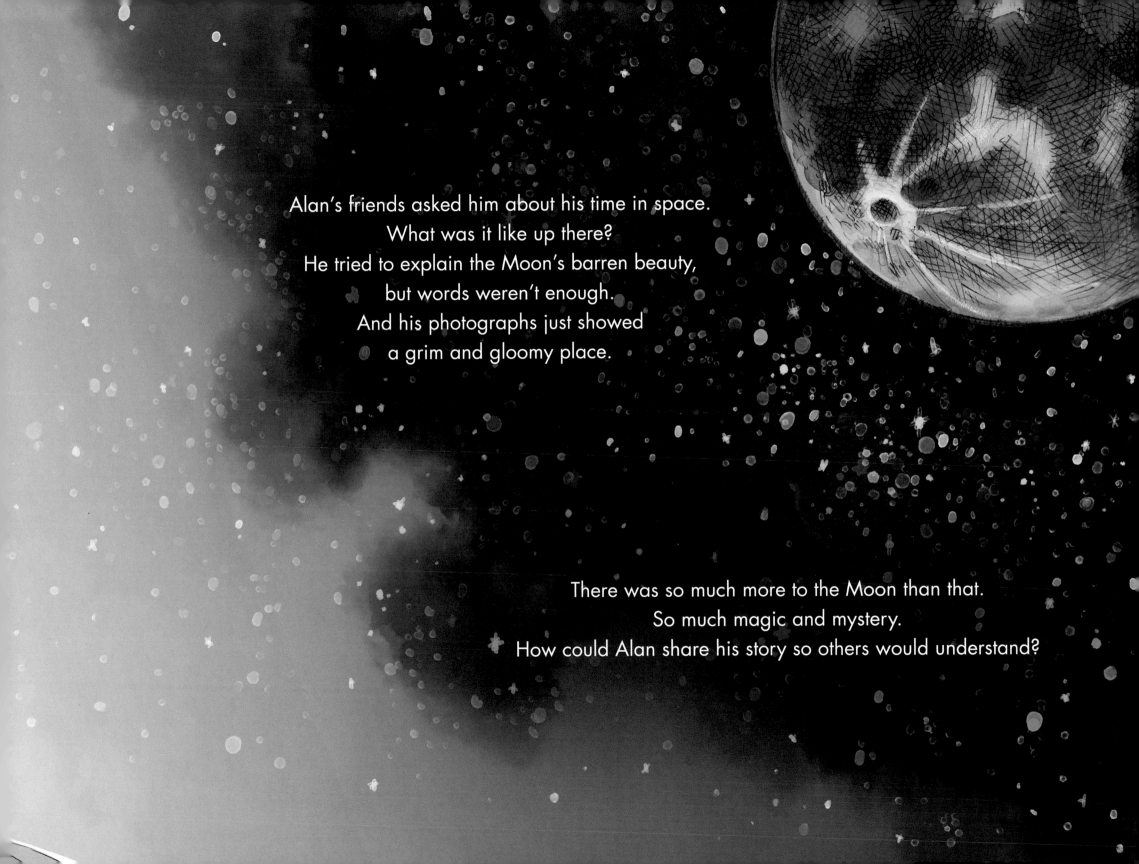

Alan's friends asked him about his time in space.
What was it like up there?
He tried to explain the Moon's barren beauty,
but words weren't enough.
And his photographs just showed
a grim and gloomy place.

There was so much more to the Moon than that.
So much magic and mystery.
How could Alan share his story so others would understand?

He pulled out his paints and brushes.
Alan knew he was the only artist ever to leave the Earth.
The only artist ever to see the Moon up close.
Maybe a painting could show how it felt to be in outer space?

Alan began his work like a scientist.
He built a model of the Moon's surface and used an electric light as the Sun.
The model helped him paint the angles and shadows just right.

Then Alan let his imagination take over.
He added red and purple to the gray dust.
Blue and green to the black craters.
Yellow and orange to the white sunlight.

The Moon didn't look exactly real,
but Alan didn't want it to.
The painting showed how stunning
outer space looked through his eyes.
How it made him feel.

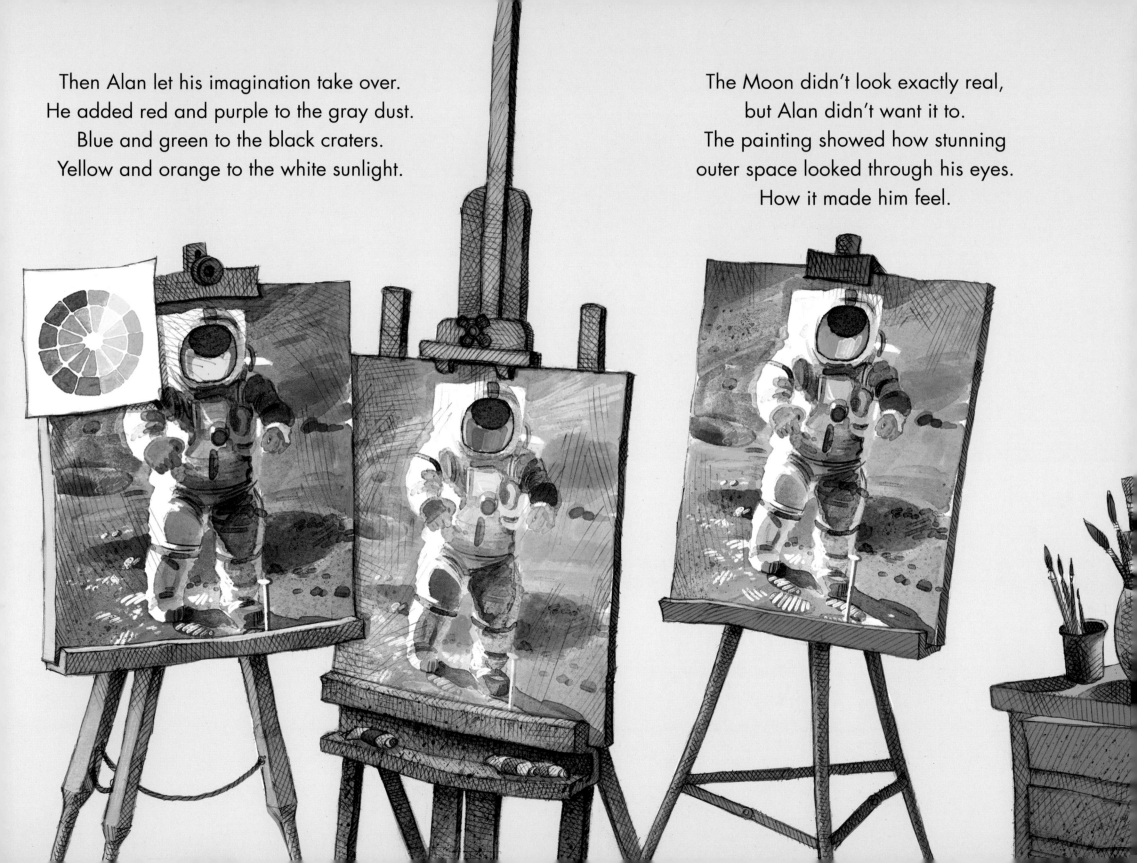

He hoped others would
feel the same thing.
The wonder of walking
on a new world.

Alan liked his Moon painting so much he did another one.
And another.
And another after that.
He mixed even brighter, bolder colors on his palette.

Could he add real pieces of outer space to his paintings?
Alan tried stamping them with astronaut boots.
He scratched them with tools he'd used on the Moon.
He sprinkled dust from his spacesuit onto the wet paint.
The surfaces grew as rough and rugged as the Moon itself.

A museum displayed
Alan's paintings for everyone to see.
Other astronauts came to remember their
own awesome adventures in space.

Boys and girls came, too.
They marveled at the shapes and colors.
They felt the wonder of walking on a new world.

Some dreamed of being
brave astronauts themselves one day.

Others dreamed of being great artists.

And some dreamed of being both.

Alan Bean (1932–2018) grew up loving airplanes. He also loved making beautiful things, beginning with the model planes he hung in his bedroom. He took his first painting class in 1961, at the same time that he trained to be a daring navy pilot.

In 1963, the National Aeronautics and Space Administration (NASA) chose Bean as an astronaut for the new United States space program. After six years of intense physical and scientific training, he traveled to the Moon with the Apollo 12 mission. On November 19, 1969, he became only the fourth person to walk on the lunar surface.

Bean returned home to a hero's welcome, with a parade in his honor and congratulations from the president of the United States. He flew another mission into space but left NASA in 1981 to work on his paintings. While other astronauts were pilots and scientists, Alan was also an artist—the only one who'd traveled to another world. In his paintings, he hoped to show what it looked like through his eyes.

Science had sent people to the Moon, but Alan knew that art could express how it felt to be up there.

Bean's paintings combined his skills as a scientist and an artist. He used exact measurements for the details, but he also used imagination to capture the dizzying sensation of walking on the Moon. By sprinkling his paintings with moon dust, scraping them with moon tools, and stamping them with moon boots, he tried to make a direct connection with his experiences in space.

As I worked with Alan on this book, I saw how much he valued sharing these experiences with a new generation. By then he was in his 80s, a time when he could have simply rested on his laurels as one of 12 humans to walk on the Moon. Instead, he generously offered to help with the story and to contribute examples of his paintings. I could tell he was passionate about showing young readers what he saw on his fantastic voyage beyond Earth's orbit.

"I think of myself not as an astronaut who paints," Alan said, "but as an artist who was once an astronaut."

This photo of Alan Bean driving a core sample tube into the lunar surface was taken during the Apollo 12 mission on November 20, 1969.

This photo of Alan Bean, taken by Pete Conrad during the Apollo 12 mission, shows Alan collecting some lunar soil to take back to Earth.

This partial view of Earth with Australia on the horizon was taken by the Apollo 12 crew.

PHOTOGRAPHS

ALAN'S PAINTINGS

"I VIVIDLY REMEMBER standing near Halo Crater and hammering this core tube into the Moon. Later, back on Earth, we would find out that, although there was some change in grain size and color, the granular material remained remarkably consistent with depth."

—Alan Bean

"WHEN I LOOK AT this painting now, I think it has some of the most beautiful color harmonies I've ever created."

—Alan Bean

"AS I LOOKED OUT my small triangular-shaped forward window, I could see the sharply curved horizon. We indeed were orbiting a body much smaller than the Earth. As I looked, the Earth, some 239,000 miles away now, appeared to rapidly rise. Australia was just coming into view. It was breathtaking."

—Alan Bean

Beginning in the 1950s, the United States (US) and the Soviet Union (USSR) competed in "The Space Race," with each country trying to outdo the other in spaceflight.

Pioneer 4 spacecraft

Astronaut John Glenn and the Mercury *Friendship 7* spacecraft

---

1

The USSR launches the first artificial satellite, *Sputnik 1*, into Earth orbit.

October 4 1957

3

The National Aeronautics and Space Administration (NASA) begins operations in the US.

October 1 1958

5

USSR cosmonaut Yuri Gagarin becomes the first human to orbit Earth in *Vostok 3KA*.

April 12 1961

7

In a special address, American president John F. Kennedy says these famous words: "I believe that this nation should commit itself to achieving the goal, before this decade is out, of landing a man on the Moon and returning him safely to the Earth."

May 25 1961

9

NASA retrieves the first data from another planet— Venus—from US spacecraft *Mariner 2*.

December 14 1962

11

Soviet cosmonaut Aleksey Leonov is the first man to walk in space.

March 18 1965

13

American astronauts Roger Chaffee, Virgil Grissom, and Edward White lose their lives in a fire during a preflight test for Apollo 1.

January 27 1967

15

US mission Apollo 11 lands on the Moon at 4:18 p.m. EST, with astronauts Edwin "Buzz" Aldrin and Neil Armstrong in the lunar module. Armstrong becomes the first person to walk on the Moon.

July 20 1969

17

US spacecraft *Mariner 9* becomes the first to orbit another planet, Mars.

November 13 1971

19

US spacecraft *Pioneer 10* becomes the first to fly by Jupiter.

December 3 1973

21

US spacecraft *Pioneer 11* is the first to fly by Saturn.

September 1 1979

2

November 3 1957

The USSR launches the first animal into space, a dog named Laika.

4

March 3 1959

The US launches *Pioneer 4*, its first spacecraft to escape Earth's gravity and fly past the Moon.

6

May 5 1961

Astronaut Alan B. Shepard, Jr., becomes the first American in space.

8

February 20 1962

American astronaut John Glenn circles Earth three times in the Mercury *Friendship 7* spacecraft.

10

June 16 1963

Soviet cosmonaut Valentina Tereshkova becomes the first woman in space on *Vostok 6*.

12

February 3 1966

USSR spacecraft *Luna 9* is the first to soft-land on the Moon.

14

December 24 1968

Apollo 8 becomes the first US mission to orbit the Moon, arriving on Christmas Eve. A message from astronauts Bill Anders, Frank Borman, and Jim Lovell is broadcast live, along with pictures of Earth

---

16

November 19 1969

US mission Apollo 12 is the second to land on the Moon, with astronauts Alan Bean and Pete Conrad in the lunar module.

18

December 2 1971

USSR spacecraft *Mars 3* becomes the first to soft-land on Mars.

20

July 17 1975

USSR and US spacecraft dock in space to carry out the first international space mission, the Apollo-Soyuz Test Project.

Mariner 9 spacecraft

Voyager 2

Hubble Space Telescope

Image of Mercury from *MESSENGER*

Astronaut Guy Bluford becomes the first African American in space on the space shuttle *Challenger*.

August 30 1983

23

Franklin Chang Díaz becomes the first Hispanic American in space on the space shuttle *Columbia*.

January 12 1986

25

Seventy-three seconds after liftoff, space shuttle *Challenger* explodes, killing the entire crew, including astronauts Greg Jarvis, Christa McAuliffe, Ron McNair, Ellison Onizuka, Judy Resnik, Dick Scobee, and Michael Smith.

January 28 1986

27

Hubble Space Telescope launches.

April 24 1990

29

Ellen Ochoa becomes the first Hispanic woman in space on the space shuttle *Discovery*.

April 8 1993

31

US spacecraft *Galileo* is the first to orbit Jupiter.

December 7 1995

33

First expedition of the International Space Station.

October 31 2000

35

The first US spacecraft lands on an asteroid.

February 12 2001

37

The space shuttle *Columbia* breaks apart upon reentering Earth's atmosphere, killing astronauts Michael Anderson, David Brown, Kalpana Chawla, Laurel Clark, Rick Husband, William McCool, and Ilan Ramon, approximately 16 minutes prior to the scheduled landing.

February 1 2003

39

Cassini-Huygens lander touches down on Saturn's largest moon, Titan.

January 14 2005

41

US spacecraft *MESSENGER* is the first to orbit Mercury.

March 17 2011

43

22

June 18 1983

Astronaut Sally Ride becomes

24

January 24 1985

Ellison Onizuka becomes the first

26

January 14 1986

US spacecraft *Voyager 2* is

28

August 24 1989

Voyager 2 is the first spacecraft to

30

September 12 1992

Mae Jemison becomes the

32

February 3 1995

Eileen Collins becomes the first

34

May 2 1997

Kalpana Chawla becomes the first

36

November 2 2000

The first US and Russian resident

38

November 23 2002

John Herrington becomes the first

40

July 1 2004

The joint US, Italian, and

42

October 10 2007

Peggy Whitson becomes the

Bibliography:

Bean, Alan, and Andrew Chaikin. *Apollo: An Eyewitness Account*. Seymour, CT: The Greenwich Workshop Press, 1998.

Bean, Alan. *My Life As an Astronaut*. New York: Aladdin Books, 1988.

Bean, Alan. *Painting Apollo: First Artist on Another World*. Washington, DC: Smithsonian Books, 2009.

Beattie, Donald A. *Taking Science to the Moon: Lunar Experiments and the Apollo Program*. Baltimore: Johns Hopkins University Press, 2003.

Dempsey, Amy. *Styles, Schools, and Movements: The Essential Encyclopaedic Guide to Modern Art*. London, UK: Thames & Hudson, 2011.

Doss, Erika. *Twentieth-Century American Art*. Oxford, UK: Oxford University Press, 2002.

Grant, R.G. *Flight: The Complete History*. London, UK: DK Publishing, 2007.

Murray, Charles, and Catherine Bly Cox. *Apollo: The Race to the Moon*. New York: Simon & Schuster, 1989.

Dedications:

To Alan Bean, for his kindness and generosity. —Dean Robbins

For Sammy and Charlie, in memory of Tom Wolfe and Alan Bean. —Sean Rubin

Acknowledgments:

Thank you to Orli Zuravicky for her editorial wizardry and to Marietta Zacker for her many talents. —D.R.

ISBN 978-1-338-25953-7

10 9 8 7 6 5 4 3 2 1   19 20 21 22 23

Printed in China 62   First edition, June 2019
The text type was set in Futura. The display type was set in DragonTS.
Book design by Kirk Benshoff

"It is my dream that on the wings of my paintbrush many people will see what I saw and feel what I felt, walking on another world some 240,000 miles from my studio here on planet Earth."

—Alan Bean

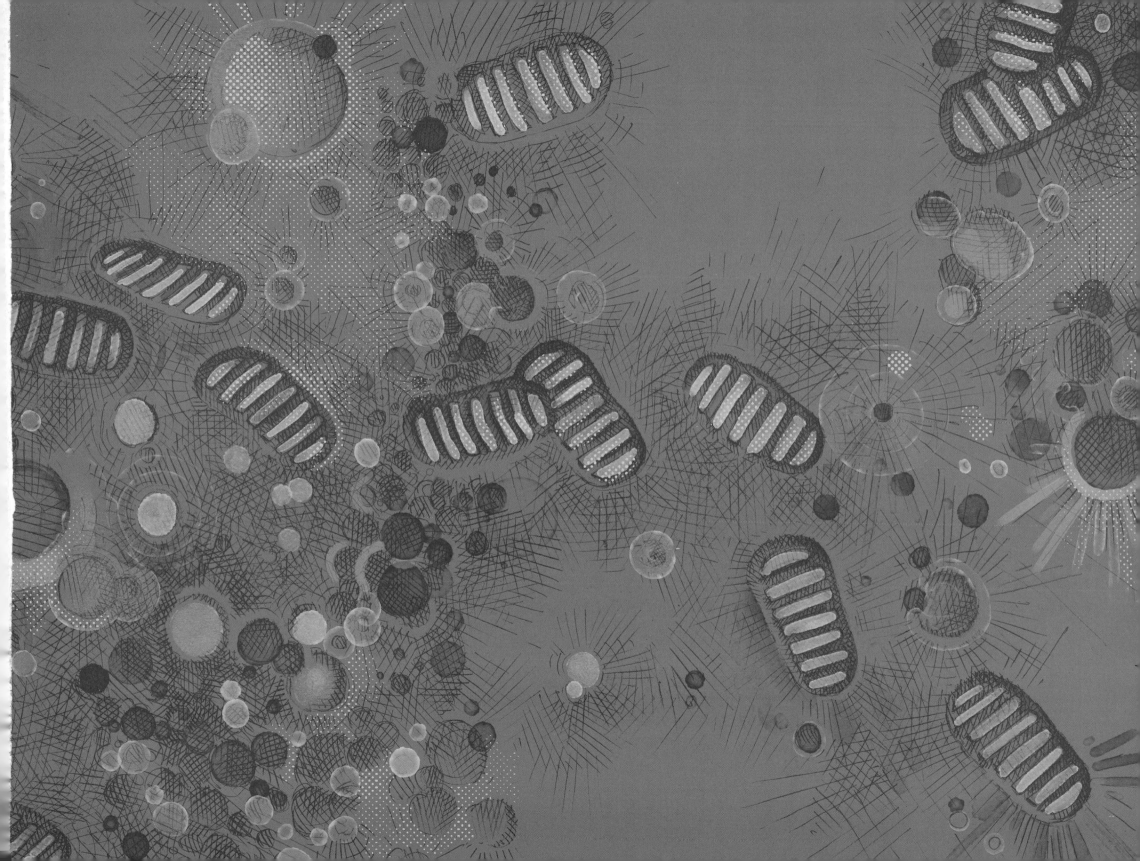

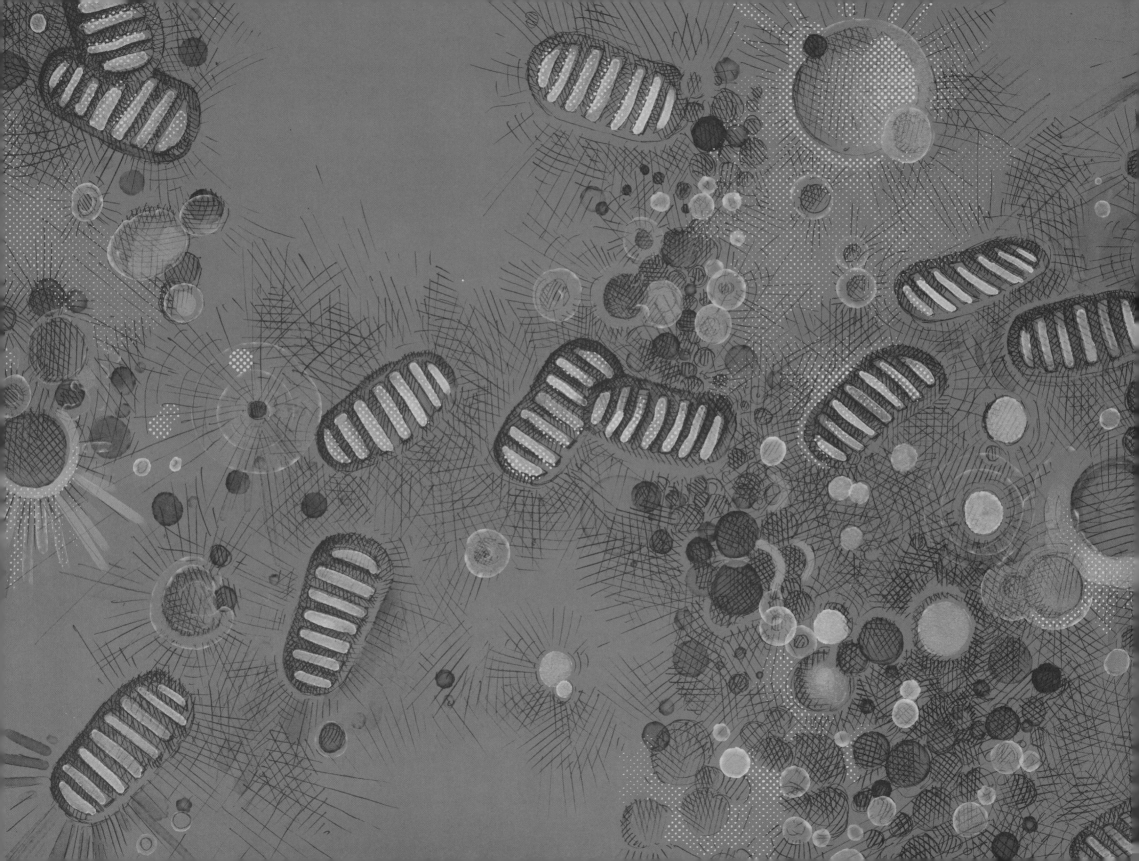